Saving Money

The Top 100 Best Ways
To Save Your Money
And To Spend Your Money Wisely

By Ace McCloud
Copyright © 2014

Disclaimer

The information provided in this book is designed to provide helpful information on the subjects discussed. This book is not meant to be used, nor should it be used, to diagnose or treat any medical condition. For diagnosis or treatment of any medical problem, consult your own physician. The publisher and author are not responsible for any specific health or allergy needs that may require medical supervision and are not liable for any damages or negative consequences from any treatment, action, application or preparation, to any person reading or following the information in this book. Any references included are provided for informational purposes only. Readers should be aware that any websites or links listed in this book may change.

Table of Contents

DEDICATED TO THOSE WHO ARE PLAYING THE GAME OF LIFE TO

WIN

KEEP ON PUSHING AND NEVER GIVE UP!

Ace McCloud

Be sure to check out my website for all my Books and Audio books.

www.AcesEbooks.com

Introduction

I want to thank you and congratulate you for buying the book, "Saving Money: The Top 100 Best Ways To Save Your Money And To Spend Your Money Wisely."

Have you ever lost sleep at night worrying about whether you have enough money? Are you up to your neck in debt and are unsure of what to do so that you can finally start saving money for yourself? Do you worry about what you're going to do in the event of a financial emergency? Are you guilty of impulse purchases? Most of all, do you want to be in control of your finances? If so, there's no need to be stressed out anymore. Stop wondering what happens to all of your money and start watching it grow right before your eyes using the information, strategies and techniques in this book!

When you're in control of your finances, you won't have to worry about living "paycheck to paycheck", as many people do today. Best of all, you won't have to live on such a tight budget. By taking charge of your money, you will find that you may have more money to do leisurely things or have all the "extras" that you want, such as nice dinners out or that new jacket you've been eying at the mall. You can even save up enough money to make a big life purchase, like a rental house or a sports car. When you have enough money, you won't be afraid to look at your monthly bank statements and you'll feel great knowing that you've mastered one of the most difficult and important areas of your life!

So what does it take to achieve financial freedom? By learning how to save and spend your money wisely, you can easily make progress toward your financial goals. This book contains proven steps and strategies on how to make the best investments in yourself, eliminate debt and start saving money. In each chapter, you will learn the best tricks and tips on how to improve your budget so that you keep more of it yourself each month. You will also learn how to make smart investments so that you can stop working for your money and have your money start working for you!

No matter what your income is, whether it is stable or erratic, high or low, stop worrying about your finances by taking intelligent action towards your financial goals. Just by implementing a few of the strategies in this book, you could see a huge difference in your financial well-being. Stop looking at wealthy people and feeling jealous—because you can and you *will* achieve the feeling of being "wealthy," too one day!

Chapter 1: Investing in YOURSELF

So what *should* you spend money on? One of the first things that you should invest in is yourself because being able to save money starts with **you**. The better health you are in, physically and mentally, the better you can perform at anything! Besides health, you should also make it a priority to live in a good environment, have strong relationships, and have the willpower to get into some great habits, and that includes spending habits! You will learn more on how to sharpen your spending habits later on, but for now, I will share with you the importance of investing in self-improvement.

Self-Improvement

I believe that you can never improve yourself enough. There is always room to learn something new and there is always a way to get better at something you're really good at. When it comes to spending money, it is important to pay your bills, but the next thing that you should focus on is putting money towards self-improvement. This includes your physical health, mental health, and education.

Physical Health. The healthier you are physically, the less likely you are to develop illnesses and ailments and you'll also have a higher chance of living a longer, happier life. In a way, money can't buy that feeling of success, but if you pay attention to what you do put your money towards, your chances of reaching financial freedom can be much greater.

- First things first, it is important to eat a healthy, balanced diet. Eating out sometimes as a treat or for a special occasion is okay, but if you do your own grocery shopping and learn how to cook, you can save money while spending money and improve your physical health all at the same time. Pay special attention to what you are buying and focus on getting plenty of fruits, vegetables, whole grains and protein.

- Secondly, invest some time and money into exercise. You can purchase your own home gym equipment or get a gym membership. If you're not looking to invest money into exercise, you can simply exercise outdoors. Just 20-30 minutes of walking a day is great for you! Adding exercise to eating a healthy diet is key for maintaining a healthy weight and keeping your immune system in tip-top shape.

- Third, get plenty of sleep! If you do not get enough sleep for your age, your body will not be able to function as well. The less productive you are, the less likely you are to accomplish successful things. Invest in some good shut-eye time and your body *and* wallet will thank you!

- Make regular doctor's appointments to make sure that you are doing everything correctly. Your doctor can help you figure out if your body has any deficiencies and if you should make any changes to your eating and exercise plan based off your individual health situation. Some people have vitamin/mineral deficiencies and will need to take supplements.

For more advanced information on how to get healthy and increase your energy levels, be sure to check out my best-selling books: Ultimate Health Secrets and Ultimate Energy.

Mental Health. Your mental health is just as important as your physical health. Investing in this area should also be a high priority. Mental stress and depression can make you care less about your spending willpower and you are more likely to feel horrible about yourself overall. Here are some great ways to invest in your mental health and some of these strategies won't even cost you anything but time.

- **Practice yoga.** Yoga can be a very relaxing type of exercise and you can do it by yourself or with a group. Scientifically, yoga manipulates your body's stress response system, meaning that it can help offset anxiety-related issues such as increased heartbeat and can help make you less sensitivity to pain. A wise investment would be to take a class or buy a DVD that teaches you the basics of yoga. You can also check out this YouTube video posted by BeFiT for a nice yoga routine: Jillian Michaels: Yoga Meltdown Level 1.

- **Meditate.** People have used meditation as an anti-stress technique for centuries. It can help you get in touch with your body, your thoughts, nature, or anything else. It is a very relaxing technique that you can perform in any dark, quiet room. Best of all, the only resource you need to invest into meditation is time.

- **Try Aromatherapy.** Aromatherapy can be very relaxing for some people, as certain scents can help your body release stress and anxiety. A wise investment would be to buy a small oil diffuser and try a few different scented oils to combat stress. I have found that lavender, patchouli, valerian root, chamomile, and eucalyptus oils work best for anti-anxiety and relaxation.

I have written many other books that are aimed at improving specific areas of your physical and mental health. For physical health improvement, you can learn a lot from my books Ultimate Health Secrets, Ultimate Energy, Vegetarian Diet, Laughter and Humor Therapy, and many body-specific books such as my Back Pain Treatment book. In terms of mental health, my library consists on books that can help you exert more willpower as well as feel more inspired, motivated, and creative. I have also written on great pro-mental health topics such as forgiveness, massage therapy, and how to overcome fear. For a complete list of my collection, please check out my website here.

Environment and Relationships

Another area of self-improvement that you should invest your resources into is your environment and relationships. You can be in the best health ever but if your environment and relationships are not in tune with it, then you probably won't get very far.

As far as your environment goes, one of the most important things you can do is keep it clean. Clutter is known to actually cause more stress, so if you live in an organized place, you are less likely to be stressed out and more likely to be productive. Invest some time into cleaning up and you'll find yourself feeling great! Do your best to organize everything into neat little areas that are easy to access and well-organized. If you live in a nice outdoors area, take advantage of that and go for strolls in your local parks. If you live in a more industrial area, such as a city, go out, get involved, and make the most out of your life and living arrangement. The friendlier you are with people, the more likely you are to make friends. You can even increase your chances of getting great job opportunities just by talking to people.

That brings us to the topic of relationships. If you are are missing great, strong, healthy relationships in your life, you're physical and mental health risk the chance of decreasing. The key is to surround yourself with positive, supportive, and like-minded people. Negative people will only bring you down. Invest some time into developing good relationships with your friends and loved ones. The stronger they are, the stronger you can be.

Education

Finally, one of the best things that you can do to improve your life is to invest in your own education. Whether you spend $100,000 to go to a well-known university (we'll get to overcoming your debt problems later), or just $10-25 on books and materials each month for personal education, you can't go wrong. I know a lot of people who have been out of school for years yet they continue to read and learn because it fulfills them and it helps them become better people. I think it's very easy and wise to make monetary investments into your overall self-improvement because you could gain something truly valuable to apply to your life that will pay huge dividends for you throughout the rest of your life. The more you learn, the more that you will find doors of opportunity opening for you. Learning new things can help you feel confident, inspired, and motivated to do great things with your life. Also, the more you learn, the more job opportunities you can get along with great ideas that could earn you or save you lots of money.

The point of this chapter is that investing in yourself is crucial for being successful at *anything*. All of the points listed in this chapter can easily make up the foundation of a great, successful life. By investing your time and money into these things, your chance of a higher return in your life can increase. For example, if you spend $10 a month on general self-improvement books, you may find that it's easier to talk to others, be confident, and be motivated, which may lead to a promotion at your job or the courage to follow a lifelong dream. Now that you know the importance of self-investment, let's move on to Chapter 2 where you will begin to learn about the importance of saving money.

Chapter 2: The Best Ways To Save and Pay Off Debt

Before you learn about the different ways to save and spend your money, it is important to understand the importance of saving. Since many people have trouble making the decision to save or pay off debt, you will also learn the reasons why you need to make this a priority in your life.

Build a Savings Account

The two most common types of checking accounts that most people have are checking and savings accounts. By keeping money in a checking account, you can gain easy access to that money for spending by writing out a check or swiping a debit card. A savings account is a little different. Many people put money into a savings account for the purposes of, obviously, saving. You might open a savings account to save money for emergencies, retirement, or a down payment for a large asset. Money that you put into a savings account acquires interest over a period of time. Best of all, you don't need a large amount of money to start a savings account. Depending on your bank, you might only need as much as $25 to begin. Some banks charge a low monthly fee or offer them for free to open a savings account and interest rates will vary by bank. Always shop around before deciding on a bank to open a savings account with. You should generally be able get one for free.

There are many benefits to opening a savings account. First and foremost, your chances of spending that money are much less than if your money was in a checking account. Secondly, your money is safe in a savings account. If your house were ever to get burglarized, or if a tornado ripped through your neighborhood and swept your house away, your money would still be safe and sound in the bank. Money in a savings account is also safe because it is insured by the FDIC if you live in the USA. So if your bank were to close, you wouldn't lose your money. Finally, many people open savings accounts to accrue interest. That is when your bank *pays* you money to lend your money. When that happens, your bank will usually pay you interest every month.

Basic savings accounts, which usually only require small fees to get started, only earn a small amount of interest each month. A market money account gains a higher amount of interest but often has limitations. For example, you need a lot of money to put into it and you can only make a small amount of withdrawals.

Once you've opened your savings account, your bank will give you a log where you can track your money. You can also track your deposits, withdrawals, fees, and interest gains by reading your monthly statements. To learn a little bit more on the different types of savings accounts that your bank may offer you, check out this YouTube video, <u>Money Management: Types of Savings Accounts</u> by ehowfinance.

Investing Your Money

Besides opening a savings account and letting the bank lend out your money, there are many other smart ways to invest your money. This section will give an overview of the different types of investing. Many people are turned away from the idea of investment because it can often be a risky venture. However, as long as you go into it with knowledge and goals, your chances of being successful can be higher.

Invest in Property

Many people who invest in property for business purposes usually make a great profit in the long-run. For example, if you buy a car for $25,000 and use it as a taxi cab, you can pay the investment off in 5 years if you bring in $5,000 a year. Then, after 5 years, you can make a profit for as long as you operate the cab. If you buy a home for $100,000 and rent it out at $2,000 a month, you can make your money back in roughly 4 and half years as well as a $24,000/year profit after the investment is paid off.

Real estate investments are great ideas because with the right strategy, they can make you thousands of dollars and require little work, depending on how you invest, your tenants and what the condition of the property is.

Invest in Other Businesses

Investing in another business allows you to share part of the profit. For example, if you make a 50% investment in a skateboard shop and the shop makes $10,000 after expenses, you will receive $5,000 of that money. This type of investment can be a little risky.

Capital Gain Incomes

Capital gain incomes is a very simple type of investment. A capital gain income is when you go out and buy something at one price and then turn around and sell it for a higher price. The difference between the price you bought it at and the price you sold it at is your capital gain. This is a great strategy when you flip a property, buy and resell products, or start and sell businesses.

Invest in Stocks

Investing in stocks is another great method of investment, although it can be risky, such as investing in a business. The two different types of stocks are called preferred stock and common stock. Preferred stock is best for those who don't get excited by risk taking because the price of the stock doesn't tend to fluctuate. Shareholders also get paid dividends through preferred stock. So if a company were to go bankrupt, preferred stock holders would have a priority over common stock holders. Common stock is more risky but its return potential is much higher.

It is important to pay attention to supply and demand when dealing with stocks. The better a company does, the more people will want to own a share of stock for that company. In accordance with supply and demand, the price of the stock will go up as more people want it. If you choose to sell that stock when the demand goes up, you'll make a profit.

Here are some great visual resources that you can use for more information on investing in stocks:

Stock Market For Beginners – Advice by Warren Buffet
Warren Buffet: How Should the Average Person Invest in the Stock Market?

Invest in Bonds

When investors loan money to businesses and the government, they issue a bond when the money they need is too much to get from a bank. By investing in bonds, the organization that sells bonds (the bond issuer) will charge the buyer an interest rate. By lending out your personal money you will be able to collect that interest rate over time. Bondholders have first priority when bankruptcy hits and are much less riskier than investing in stocks.

Here are some great visual resources that you can use for more information on investing in bonds:

How Bond Investing Works
The Basics of Bonds

Real Estate. Many people buy real estate properties for as little as possible, put money into restoring them, and then resell them for a profit. You can also invest in a Real Estate Investment Trust (REIT), which is when you buy a percentage of a company that operates real estate, such as an apartment complex.

Assets. One way to double your money and then some is to make an investment in a piece of property that can drive money. For example, if you bought a school bus for $20,000 and you used it for a transportation business; you could make your money back in 4 years if you can make a profit of at least $4,000 a year. Once you have your money back, the rest of the profit becomes money that you didn't have before.

Saving vs. Paying Off Debt

Most expert financial advisers agree that you should save between 10 to 20% of your income. However, the actual rate of savings for the majority of the United States is only 4.2%. Why is that? It's because many U.S. Citizens are piled up to their necks in debt. The most common type of debt is credit card debt. Many people find themselves in bad credit card debt because credit cards easily bring on feelings of instant gratification. That brings many people to the question of, "Should I focus on saving or on paying off my debt?" While it is important to save, paying off high-interest debts as fast as you can should be your first priority.

As always, here is an example that may help you understand this better:

Let's pretend that you have a $10,000 credit card debt with a 15% interest rate. The bank requires a minimum payment of 1% of the principal balance plus interest. That means your minimum payment per month is $225. Breaking it down even further, you would see that $100 of that goes toward your principal and the other $125 goes straight to the bank for interest. If you were to continue paying off that debt using the monthly minimum amount, it would take you nearly 30 years to pay it *and* it would cost you $12,000 just in interest!

Let's look at it in a different scenario: Say now you can pay $400 a month toward that debt. You'd be able to pay off your debt in just two years and you would save $10,000 in interest if you saved what you'd normally pay for 5 years. So instead of losing all of your money to the bank, you'd still have it, just in a saving's account.

The best benefit that comes with paying off your debt is that you will have a guaranteed rate of return on your money. You'll be out of debt sooner than you know and you won't have to pay so much in interest. However, you should save a small amount of money before you start paying off your debts, just in case an emergency arises. A good goal would be to save for at least 5-6 months of living expenses before you start putting money toward your debt.

Debt is not just limited to credit cards. Many people are in debt with their student loans and mortgages, among other loans. Here are some other great strategies than can help you offset your debt and have more to save in the future:

The Stacking Method. For this method, make a list of all of your debts, starting with the one that has the highest interest rate. For any credit card debt, shop around and try to transfer it to another bank for a lower interest rate. Once you have done that, re-rank your debts again. Next, take out your budget and see if you can make adjustments. For any money that you can shave off your regular bills, put it toward paying off your highest debt while also paying the minimum repayments on your other debts.

Snowball Method. For this method, make a list of all of your debts and include the current balance for each. Find the debt that has the smallest balance and cut as many costs from your budget as possible to add to the minimum monthly payment. You'll pay that debt off quicker than you'd thought and then you can move on to the next smallest payment and repeat the process until all of your debt is out the door.

Debt Settlement. In some cases, you may be able to use a professional debt arbitrator to get a lower outstanding balance. The arbitrator will negotiate with creditors to settle on an amount that is more affordable for you to pay off.

Debt Consolidation. This is similar to debt settlement except professionals will negotiate with creditors to lower your principal balance and then consolidate your debt with the highest interest into one monthly payment with a lower interest rate. A lot of people will do this on a refinance of their mortgage. In some cases this can be very beneficial, and other cases it may not be wise. It is also easy to go off and start spending a lot of money once a debt consolidation has been completed. This is exactly what you do not want to do. Be sure to show some discipline and spend wisely.

Chapter 3: Simple Ways To Save Money

Now that you know what to do in order to get a handle on your finances, it is time to learn about little, easy things you can do to save money. Sometimes, saving money is as easy as making a simple switch or thinking about your alternative options. You will learn some great ways on how to simply save money in this chapter!

Go to the Library. As you probably know, books can be very expensive, especially textbooks. In most cases, your local library may have the same book that you could buy in a store. Library memberships are often cheap or free and can be used an unlimited amount of times—you could even stay there and read all day if you wanted. Going to the library is a fun activity and best of all; it's much cheaper than buying brand new books in the store.

Pick Nature Over Electronics. Instead of spending endless money on electronics, which often sucks your money (let's face it—Microsoft and Sony are always getting you with those add-on expansion packs or super cool new gadget/game), put your wallet way and go enjoy something free—nature! It's better than video games or being online because you can enjoy fresh air, watch animals, and exercise in a fun way. It's also family friendly and you can enjoy nature almost anywhere! Best of all, it's free!

Explore Your Own Backyard. Instead of planning lavish vacations in tourist spots, which are almost guaranteed to suck your money away, plan a "staycation" and check out the local scene. Often times, there are amazing, cheap things to do in your own town that you never knew existed. See if your area has any great museums, historical sites, parks, natural trails etc. Having a staycation means that you will spend less on travel and hotel-fare and if you're lucky, you'll discover some cheap and fun things to do right in your own backyard.

Avoid Mall Without Money. Don't even think about going to the mall unless you have extra spending money. How many times have you tagged along with a friend "just to look" or "just to go along" and ended up buying something that you saw and wanted? Often times, that happens to people who don't plan on spending money, so it usually comes right out of their pay for the month. Shopping anywhere without money is usually dangerous for your wallet, so only try to go when you actually have an allotted amount of "recreational shopping" funds or simply save it for a special reward or treat later on.

Record Shows and Skip Through Commercials to Avoid Spending Urges. When watching commercials, your chances of being tempted to buy something can highly increase, thanks to marketers. To avoid risking the urge of spending from commercials, record your favorite TV shows in advance and watch them later. This way, you can fast forward through the commercials. I almost never watch TV live anymore! When I was younger I would be forced to sit through who knows how many hours of different commercials. Modern day technology truly is incredible when used wisely!

Clip Coupons. Taking a few hours to clip coupons can end up saving you a good amount of money each month. I have found that the best time to clip coupons is on Sunday, as many stores' sales run Sunday to Sunday. Around my area, they usually send out their coupons in the newspaper each Sunday.

Shop at Thrift Stores and Garage Sales. Shopping at thrift stores and garage sales can net you a lot of really cool things for super cheap! Contrary to popular belief, you can find a lot of almost-new items this way and the fun part is that you never know what you will find. At my local thrift shop, you can get all sorts of cool items for $3 or less. Sometimes you can even find clothes that still have the tags on them! What's better than scoring a name-brand clothing item for a fraction of the price?

Buy Safe Used Cars From Individuals. Instead of buying a used car from a dealership try looking around to see if you can buy one from an individual seller. Car dealerships often try to sell you those "extras" such as extended warranties or cleaning services which will rack up your total bill. If you choose to finance a car through a dealership, you will still get hit with a couple hundred dollars of interest in the long-run. If possible, shop around before heading to a dealership. You can usually find good deals from individual sellers in your local newspaper classifieds or on Craigslist. This, however is a risky proposition. If you're lucky you'll save thousands of dollars in the long run, and if you're unlucky it could cost you thousands of dollars. My actual personal preference is to buy new cars that are known for quality and to just take really good care of them so that they last a very long time.

Only Eat Out for Special Occasions. While it may be tempting to eat out so that you don't have to cook yourself, eating out too much can definitely add up and squeeze your hard-earned money out of your pocket. A better way to save money is to save eating out for special occasions or just set one night aside to get take-out. Your overall health and energy levels will also thank you!

Learn to Cook. That being said, learning how to cook can save you a lot of money, especially if you combine this idea with coupon clipping. One of the best benefits of learning how to cook is that one dish can often last you several days if you get creative and utilize the leftovers. You'll get a lot more value for your money and if you pay attention to your shopping list, you can eat a much more balanced diet.

Take Care of Personal Possessions (toys, cars, lawn, etc). By taking care of your personal possessions, you can make them last longer, therefore getting more value out of your money. Take care of everything that you have. Take care of your house so that it doesn't end up in need of a total makeover. Teach your children to take care of their toys so you won't be forced to buy replacements. Take care of your car so that you can have many years to come with no car payment for repairs.

Re-purpose Items. Many of your personal possessions can be re-purposed into something great and useful just when you think you no longer have a need for it. For example, you might have a special t-shirt that you wore as a child and eventually you grew out of it. One cool idea is to turn it into a pillow that you can use to decorate your house or sleep on. I've also seen a cool idea to turn your child's crib into a desk once they've outgrown it. The possibilities are endless!

Determine Whether It's Worth More to Rent or Own Something. Have you ever considered buying a boat or a motor home or something like that? Of course, those types of things can be very expensive. One option is to figure out if it is worth more to rent or buy items like those. For example, say you wanted to buy a kayak. Do you live near water? Do you travel somewhere each year that has water? If you're not going to use it a lot, it may be a better option to rent. If you determine that you're going to get a lot of usage out of it, it may be more valuable to buy.

Watch Bank Statements. A great way to better manage and save money is to keep an eye on your bank statements, especially if you let somebody else (kids, spouse, etc) use your credit and debit cards from time to time. When you use plastic and auto-debits to pay for things rather than cash, it is very easy to lose track of just how much you're spending. At the end of the month, review them. This way, you can have a good idea of how much money you're spending each month and you can see if anyone else is racking up your bills.

Cell Phone Plans. Have you reviewed your cell phone plan lately? Big-name cell phone companies like Verizon and AT & T charge high amounts for cell phone contracts that you have to lock yourself. However, there are other options that you can consider for your cell phone plan, such as Boost Mobile. Their company doesn't lock you into a contract and you can activate almost any phone for a reasonable price. Basic cell phone payments can go down to as low as $30 after you make a certain amounts of payments on time and smart phone payments can go as low to $45-50. If your cell phone bill is killing you, that might be something to look into.

Secret Menus. Save some money by learning about the "secret menu" at some restaurants. There's not really a separate secret menu, but if you know how to spot certain snags on the menu, you can save a little bit here or there. For example, Burger King once had a sandwich called the "Buck Double" and it also had the traditional double cheeseburger. The difference was one slice of cheese and $2. Some people began to get smart and ordered a Buck Double with extra cheese (which was essentially a double cheeseburger) and instead of paying the full price; they only had to pay $1.07 plus an extra 30 cents for cheese instead of $3.20. Another time, my friend showed me that she saved 50 cents by ordering an appetizer as her entree instead of ordering the entree option, which was the same thing. Analyze your local restaurant menus and see if you can save a little bit here and there.

Learn to Barter. Bartering is something that often goes right over the heads of many people. Back in history, bartering was common among many immigrants, who traded their products and services with one another for exchange in a product or service that they needed. However, bartering still exists and works today! You stand a much better chance at bartering in your locally-owned stores. For example, if you need a cake and you don't want to pay full price for it but you cut hair professionally, you could go to your local bakery and try to offer the owner a free hair cut in exchange for a cake.

Bartering can be overwhelming and challenging to those who are new, so check out these great YouTube videos for some extra skills and tips:

Bartering Websites, Bartering Online, How to Barter Trade and Swap Goods by Jordan Wexler
Barter Kings: Tips of the Trade by A&E

Keep Spare Change in Jar. Ever wonder what ever comes of all that spare change you end up with whenever you break bills? I know my spare change used to end up on the floor and in the side door of my car. However, that little change can really add up! A cool idea that you can do to save as much money as you can is to get a big jar and just drop all of your spare change into it every time you pass it. After a few months, see how much extra money you can end up saving as a result of that. You'd be surprised how much that little 30 cents here and 50 cents there can add up!

Carpool. If you and your co-workers live near each other, a good idea to save on money is to take turns carpooling to work. This way, you can save some money on gas and some mileage on your car, which will eventually cause it to need work.

Actively Ask For A Discount or Deal. You may be shocked at how much you can save if simply ask for it. I go out of my way once a year to make sure I'm getting the best deal possible on everything that I am spending money on. Some areas to focus on would be your cell phone bills, cable bills, credit cards and car insurance. Especially with the very big companies, you can usually find a customer service representative that will give you a discount on your bill. If the first person says no, try again a later time. Also, don't be afraid to ask for the manager. I harassed my cell phone provider quite a few times before I finally found a nice representative who gave me an incredible deal! I also called my cable company around five times before I got a deal so good that many say it's the best they've ever seen! Be persistent and be sure to shop around. Many companies will match discounts from other companies or give you an incentive to stay if you threaten to cancel or leave.

Chapter 4: Saving Money On Groceries and Getting the Healthiest Bang For Your Buck

Whenever I go out to the grocery store, I can't help but overhear people say things like, "If only we didn't need to eat, do you know how much money we would save?" or "Wow, that $100 really went fast!" While it is true that you cannot avoid paying for your food, it is also true that there are ways to get around the high costs of grocery shopping. You will learn some great tips on how to do that in this chapter.

Buy Skim or 2% Milk and Pay Attention to Size. The prices of milk can sometimes get pretty costly. I don't know if this rings true for everybody, but where I live, gallons of whole milk are often a couple cents more expensive than gallons of 2% and skim. 2% and skim milk are usually healthier for you anyway. Another great way to save money on milk is to be aware of how much milk you actually use. For those who go through a lot of milk, it would be better to buy gallons. However, if you use a decent amount of milk in a week but a gallon goes bad before you can use it all, check around your local stores and see what kind of deals you can get. Around me, you can get two small plastic bottles of milk for a deal and if you don't go through too much, you won't waste as much by buying smaller, therefore getting more value for your money. You can also switch to almond or rice milk, which can stay fresh for many months at a time!

Buy Lean Ground Meats and Pay Attention to Dates. While ground meats with the labels 73/27 and 80/20 are cheaper than 90/10 or 93/7, they are usually not as healthy for you. Organic ground, the best option, meat is often a couple dollars more expensive. Pay close attention to the dates on the labels. If you can find one that is going to expire within two or three days and you bring it to the manager's attention, he or she will often mark it right down for you. Grocery stores will always try to mark something down that is going bad before they count it as a total loss.

Coupons. Most grocery stores have their weekly fliers available at the entrance and many of them contain coupons. Many people don't even think to grab a flier when they walk inside. Just beware: only use a coupon if you actually need that product! Using coupons to get the best discounts can be tricky. Check out this YouTube video by vera sweeney for an expert opinion on how to get started and be successful in using coupons—How to Start Couponing: A Realistic Approach. You can also call many corporations on the phone and simply asked them to mail you coupons. The same is true for many other online retailers, you can try e-mailing them and asking them for a discount.

Buy in Bulk. When you can, buy dry grocery products in bulk, but only when it makes sense or its on sale. For example, in some stores, you can buy individual packs of Ramen noodles for 0.45 cents each but in other stores, you can buy 12 packs for $2. Before buying anything in bulk, be sure it is something that you or your family uses a lot of and it is something that will not go bad quickly.

Don't Fill Your Cart. Although it can be tempting, don't fill your shopping cart when you go grocery shopping. Make a list of exactly what you need and make a conscious decision to stick to it. You may find it helpful to use a hand basket or no shopping basket at all. The less space you have, the less you're likely to carry and overspend on! Even when you are filling your cart with low-priced items, it can be very easy to go overboard and you may end up negatively surprised at the checkout.

Review Order While Waiting in Line. While you're waiting in line, review what you've picked up and don't be afraid to put anything that you don't really need back. As you're unloading your items on the belt, ask yourself, "Do I really need this item? How will it affect my health? My family? Can we live without it?" This is a good strategy to prevent yourself from overspending on junk food and extras.

Watch Personal Care Product Prices. Personal care items such as toothpaste, toilet paper, shampoo, soap, toothbrushes, etc are often overpriced in grocery stores. Check your local pharmacies or online retailer to see if they offer them for a lower price. Some dollar stores also sell good-quality toiletries at a discounted price. For example, you can get name-brand shampoo and conditioner from a local dollar store $1.29 per bottle whereas other places will try selling the same kind of product $3.29 per bottle. The key is to keep your eye on the prices and find the best places to purchase various items that you use regularly.

Buy Private-Label and Generic. When you buy name-brand grocery products, you're usually just paying for the name. Most grocery stores offer private-label and generic products that are essentially the same thing, but much cheaper. For the best comparison, just compare the nutritional labels. If you absolutely swear by your favorite name-brand products, pick your favorite and only spend money on that one. Buy everything else generically.

Avoid Prepared/Pre-Packaged Ready-To-Eat Foods. Avoid buying any foods that are already made and ready-to-eat, such as macaroni salad. Often times, you can buy the ingredients and make it yourself. This usually yields a bigger serving size and making food fresh nearly always tastes better!

Grate Your Own Cheese. When you buy grated or shredded cheese, you're often paying for the convenience of preparation. By buying a cheap yet durable cheese grater and going for block cheese instead, you can usually save a good amount of cents. At my local grocery store, you can buy a block of mozzarella cheese for $1.99 but the bags of shredded mozzarella cost $3.29. That right there is a local savings of $1.30!

Don't Shop While You're Hungry. Going shopping while you're hungry can cause you to make more impulse purchases, therefore racking up your final bill at the checkout.

Ask About Rain Checks. Sometimes when a grocery store offers an item on sale and it runs out before the sale is over, they will issue you a rain check, which allows you to purchase the item at the sale price whenever it comes back in stock. Not all stores offer rain checks and every policy is different but it is always worth inquiring.

Use Filtered Water Instead of Bottled Water. Investing in a water filter that you can use on water that comes right out of your faucet can save you hundreds of dollars a month if you're a person or household that goes through a lot of bottled water. It's essentially the same thing and it's also doing a great favor to the environment. My favorite water filtration system is: ZeroWater.

Shop After Holidays. Shopping the day after a holiday can net you some great deals. Many grocery stores mark down holiday-themed paper products and foods, sometimes down to less than a dollar just to get rid of it. If you need anything in particular that might be floating around near a holiday, be sure to go try and snag a deal.

Freeze Excess Food. By freezing any excess food that you have already cooked, you can keep food for longer and waste less, therefore getting good value out of your money. Most fresh foods are freezable, such as meat, fruit, and vegetables. A good idea is to make an investment in vacuum-sealed freezer bags to keep your food as fresh as possible.

Eat Vegetarian. A great way to save on food is to go vegetarian a couple of nights a week. Meat and chicken can often rack up your food bill but vegetables and other vegetarian options are often much, *much* cheaper, especially if you do some price comparisons at your local grocery stores and markets. For some great ideas on vegetarian meals, I invite you to check out my book Vegetarian Diet, Recipes, and Cooking.

Chapter 5: Don't Sweat Your Wallet: Save Money By Exercising

Exercising is important for your health but it also comes with another great benefit that you probably never even heard of before—it can help you save money! This chapter will take a look at how you can save money by exercising.

Walking. When you can, walk to your destination instead of driving. Some people are so lazy that they will drive their car literally a block away. Walking is a great alternative to driving because it doesn't require gas or maintenance and it's great on the environment too. No matter where go, walking is free!

Running vs Cycling. Bikes can cost a lot of money and so can their maintenance. Running, like walking, is essentially free. The only investment you may have to make in is a nice pair of running shoes.

Invest in a Home Gym. By putting your money toward home gym equipment, you can get a better value for your money than if you purchased a gym membership. Alternatively, if you cannot fit a home gym into your living situation, exercise outside—that's always free. I personally bought a bow flex revolution many years ago along with several free weight dumbbells and can do just about any exercise with that equipment in a regular sized bedroom.

Ways Exercising Can Save You Money:

Save on Makeup. Exercising can help improve the quality of your skin and it can also make you feel great all around, therefore boosting your self-confidence. The more confident you are about yourself, your chances of wanting to use too much makeup can decrease. Makeup can be very expensive, especially when buying the popular name-brand kind, so put some time into exercising and put more money in your wallet.

Save on Medical Costs. Exercise helps keep your physical and mental health in tip-top shape. The healthier you are, the less money you may end up spending on doctors' appointments, medications and therapies. Avoid having to pay for tests, medicines, or medical emergencies by working on your health a little bit each day.

Boost Energy and Save on Caffeine. Exercising daily can help make you more energetic, thus eliminating the need to spend money on caffeinated products, which can become highly expensive. The average cup of coffee is about $2, more or less. So if you were to buy two cups of coffee every day for a month, you'd be spending $112 just on coffee! While making it at home can be cheaper, that still adds up and it can also lead to waste. Exercise instead to get your daily energy burst and put that $112 or so towards something great!

Avoid Costly-Diet Programs. Instead of putting your money towards costly diet/weight-loss programs, just focus on practicing regular exercise and eating right. You can also very inexpensively get all the information you need to lose weight in my book on Losing Weight.

Save on Medicine and Healthcare Costs. By exercising regularly, you can avoid having to pay for costly sleeping aids, antibiotics, or any other type of medication that can give your body a healthy boost. Regular exercise usually strengthens your immune system, helps you sleep better at night, and overall keeps you healthy so that you won't have to fork over money for health care.

Chapter 6: Saving Money Through Tax Deductions

Any time you are dealing with money, you can't forget about Uncle Sam, who is always looking for his slice. Many people become stressed out during tax time. However, there is one word that often shines a ray of light to those who hate tax season—tax deductions. Tax deductions can help you reduce your tax burden and in that sense you may even get more money back. This chapter will take a look at some of the most common tax deductions that you may be able to use to pay less tax and get more back.

Expenses

Moving Expenses. If you have to move for your job, you may be eligible to deduct the related moving expenses, including mileage, which can be a nice portion of money. As long as you stay at your job for 39 weeks within a year, you can take this deduction.

Student Loan Interest. If you paid for your further education by yourself, you may be eligible to deduct the interest you paid on that loan from your taxes. Eligible persons can deduct up to $2,500 of student loan interest each year.

Charitable Donations. When you make a donation to a non-profit organization, you may be able to write it off on your taxes. Even if you donate something besides money, such as clothes to the Goodwill, you can write that off too. Best of all, if you donate your time mentoring somebody, you can write off any associated costs, such as gas mileage, trip expenses, and academic expenses.

Pet Costs. This only happens if you have a service animal or if you can prove that your pets are a part of your business (example: you own a farm and your cats help you out by keeping rats away from your food). If you can claim this, go for it!

Tax Advice/Preparation Services. Yes, you can deduct the costs of having your taxes prepared for you! Whether you buy a home program to file your taxes yourself or if you have an accountant do them for you, you can write it off as long as it is more than 2% of your adjusted gross income. You can even write off paying for tax advice in the form of consultations or reading materials.

Medical Expenses. In some cases, you may be able to write-off any out-of-pocket medical expenses that are more than 10% of your income. Married couples can deduct medical expenses that go over 7.5% of their income if one or more person was born before 1949.

Business Expenses

If you own a business you may be able to write off additional business incomes to offset the high self-employment taxes. Here are some of the most common deductions that you can use against your business taxes:

Self-Employment Tax. You can deduct half of your self-employment taxes from your total profit.

Home Office Deduction. If you have a home office that you use exclusively for work, you can deduct it. Specifically, you can deduct part of your rent, your mortgage payment, utilities, property taxes, and any maintenance. A good idea is to keep a blueprint of your home office area with correct measurements in case the IRS wants more information.

Meals and Entertainment. If you meet with somebody for business purposes over a dinner or a game of golf, you can deduct 50% of the total cost from your taxes. Be sure to keep all receipts as well as a log of who you were doing business with and specifically what kind of business you were doing during that event.

Phone, Fax, Internet. If you use a phone, fax, or the Internet for business purposes, you can deduct whatever percentage of the bill you use for it. So, if you use your personal cell phone for 50% business purposes, you can deduct 50% of your monthly bill from your business taxes.

Business Loan or Credit Card Interest. Like student loan interest, you can deduct interest that you accrue on business loans or business credit cards as long as they are being used to make exclusive business purchases.

Business Vehicles. If you use your car or a business car for business-related purposes you can take deductions on the miles you drove as long as you keep accurate records. In some cases you can also deduct maintenance such as oil changes or repairs as well as car insurance and gas.

Business-Related Publications. If you're an accountant and you have a yearly subscription to an accounting magazine, you can definitely deduct that from your business taxes. No matter what you do, if you purchase publications to help keep you knowledgeable in your field, you can deduct the costs of those materials.

Chapter 7: Save Money On Your Car and Gas

Don't Fix It If It's Not Broken. If your current car is fully functioning and still safe to drive, then drive it until it's impossible or unsafe to do so. Many people buy a new car every 3 to 5 years regardless of whether their current car is still functioning. Instead of selling your current car or trading it in, just take care of it and drive it longer. A typical monthly payment on a new car can be anywhere from $250 to $500 plus interest, so if you just stay happy with your current car, you can save yourself a lot of money per month! I haven't had to make a car payment in the last six years and still love my car!

Adjust Your Insurance. If you have a brand new car it makes sense to have full coverage on it. If you're leasing or financing, you must have full coverage. However, if you have an older car, it might not make much sense to have full coverage on it, just the coverage that you need. For example, you might find it sensible to drop your collision coverage on a car that you might only be driving for a few more years.

Shop Around For Insurance. It doesn't hurt to shop around for different insurance rates even if you've already adjusted your coverage. Many insurance companies offer different rates and specials at different times of the year.

Buy After Market Products. Dealerships tend to overprice their parts and extras. You can find many aftermarket products for your car for almost half the price. Check out this YouTube video by Automotive Body Parts Association to verify that aftermarket parts are safe and of high quality: Demonstrating Safety and Quality of Aftermarket Parts.

Do Your Own Maintenance. If you can learn how to do small maintenance jobs on your car, such as changing your own oil or replacing a burned-out bulb, you can save yourself a couple of hundred dollars a year. There are many tutorials online that will show you how to do small maintenance jobs step-by-step.

Buy Gas Cards at Discounted Price. If you shop around online you may be able to find some good deals on gas cards. Some websites will sell you a $100 gas card for just $95, which means you can get a free gallon of gas at many gas stations.

Don't Drive Aggressively. Your car uses more gas when you rapidly accelerate so avoid aggressive or angry driving.

Use Cruise Control. When applicable, use your cruise control function. When your car travels at a balanced speed, it will use less gas than if you keep changing your speed.

Get Gas on Certain Days. Research shows that the best time of the week to buy gas is on Wednesday or Thursday before 10am. This is because most gas stations raise their prices on Thursday to hit weekend travelers. Try to avoid filling up your tank on the weekends at all costs.

Download Gas Apps. There are many apps you can download to your smartphone that will help you find the best gas prices in your area. GasBuddy is a really good app as well as AAA Triptik.

Don't Idle. If you let your car idle for more than a minute, you will waste more gas than if you simply restarted the engine.

Pay Cash For Gas. Some gas stations charge up to 10 cents more for gas if you're paying with a credit card. This is to offset the extra costs for credit card processing. 10 cents a gallon can really add up, so look around for gas stations that charge the same price no matter how you pay or just take out extra cash for gas.

Travel Light. Carrying an extra 250 pounds in your car can use up a lot of extra gas per mile, so be sure to travel as lightly as possible.

Chapter 8: Saving Money as a Family

When it comes to saving money, there are lots of different things that you can do to get your whole family involved! When you're running a household, it may be true that you have a tighter budget than if you were by yourself, because you're responsible for running a household of people. Luckily, there are many things you can do to manage money with your whole family.

Planning with your spouse:

Homeowners or Renters? As early as you can, plan with your spouse as to whether you are going to be homeowners or renters. The earlier you know whether you're going to be a homeowner, the earlier you can start saving and putting money toward a house. However, if you are a couple who travels often, you may find it more convenient to rent instead of buy.

How Big of a Family? Another thing you should try to plan early is how big of a family you will have. That way, you can start saving and spending money wisely in anticipation of how many mouths you will have to feed one day.

Daycare Options. When you do plan to have a child, will you or your spouse make arrangements to stay home with it or will you consider daycare as an option? Knowing this ahead of time can help you allocate money toward daycare options.

Education Options. How much do you and your spouse value the importance of education? Do you want to make an investment in your children's future education? Will you need to put money aside for private school and/or college? Summer camps? Other expenses?

Vehicles. Planning for vehicles can be a bit tricky but if you can figure it out, you're one step ahead of the game. Will it be possible for your family to only own one vehicle? If you need two cars, will you finance, lease, or buy straight out? Buy new or used? Buy from a dealership or from a private seller?

Vacations. Do you and your spouse want to take a vacation every year? If so, it is important to plan it out and figure out how much money you will need to save for each vacation. Be sure to plan on saving for travel costs, lodging costs, and spending money. Then also be sure to do your research to find the best possible deals.

Retirement Plans. Do you and/or your spouse have money going into a retirement plan? If not, it is very important to consider adjusting your budget so that you can save for retirement and medical costs on your own.

Review Insurance Policies. Having insurance is important but sometimes you can find ways to cut costs here. For example, you may be eligible for a car insurance discount just by having health insurance. Also, make sure that you truly need all of your insurance policies. For example, having life, car, and homeowner's insurance are pretty important. If you have a business, you might need to take out a small business insurance policy, but only if your products may cause a liability.

Strategies to Save Money as a Family

When your kids are aware of your budget, it can be much easier for them to understand why you make the spending decisions that you make. Here are some great ways to get the whole family involved in managing money.

Create Shared Goals. When setting your goals about money, let your kids suggest some ideas too. This way, you can get an insight about their wants, needs, and how to teach them about the reality of money. A good example of a shared goal is setting up an allowance system with your children to help them learn how to manage money on their own. Then you can start letting them buy their own things, which can teach them how to be more appreciative and responsible. As they get older, your shared goals can become more advanced and eventually help your children grow up to live free from financial struggles.

Create a Budget Plan. When creating a budget plan, do it with your whole family. This way, there are no secrets or surprises and everybody knows just how much money there is to spend. For example, if your kids ask you to buy them something and they don't understand the concept of having a budget, they may not understand when you tell them you can't buy it. If they have an idea of where the family's money is coming from and how it's being spent, it can be much easier to explain why you can't buy something.

Review Debts. Review debts together as a family. This can be a great learning experience for your children and it can help you teach them not to make the same spending mistakes that you may have made. Be sure that they understand how a credit card works and how important it is to make the payments on time. Many young kids think credit cards are just free money and then go overboard on spending later in life just to discover that they're in debt.

What You Need Vs. What You Want. Teach your kids to understand the difference between what you need and what you want. You need a roof over your head, you need food on your table, and you need clothes on your back. Depending on your family's values, you may need an advanced education. When it comes to extras, like electronics, video games, accessories, etc. teach your kids that the world will not end if they don't have those things. Teach them how to save money and calibrate their earning potential so that they can *get* those things on their own without having to make sacrifices.

Conclusion

I hope this book was able to help you to gain a better understanding of what *you* need to do to start saving money. The best way to start is by investing in yourself. Then, open a savings account if you haven't already. Pick one of the strategies that you learned about earlier to eliminate your debt and get on the road to financial freedom!

The next step is to adjust your budget by using some of the strategies listed in this book. Use whatever money you save from those adjustments and either put it in your savings account or put it towards your debts. Stick to your plan and watch your debts diminish and your savings account grow. The richest people in the world have been those who have been willing to make sacrifices early on in order to reap huge benefits later on in life! Do whatever you can to stay away from debt, make intelligent decisions, find the best deals possible, use your willpower, stay healthy, set your financial goals, invest in yourself and never give up on your dreams! After that, sit back and enjoy your financial freedom!

Finally, if you discovered at least one thing that has helped you or that you think would be beneficial to someone else, be sure to take a few seconds to easily post a quick positive review. As an author, your positive feedback is desperately needed. Your highly valuable five star reviews are like a river of golden joy flowing through a sunny forest of mighty trees and beautiful flowers! *To do your good deed in making the world a better place by helping others with your valuable insight, just leave a nice review.*

Thanks and Best of Luck

My Other Books and Audio Books
www.AcesEbooks.com

Business & Finance Books

LEADERSHIP

THE TOP 100 BEST WAYS
TO BE A GREAT LEADER

Ace McCloud

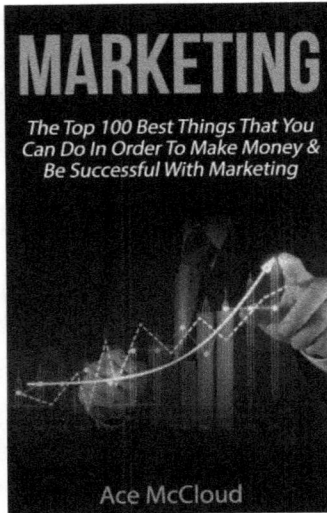

MARKETING

*The Top 100 Best Things That You
Can Do In Order To Make Money &
Be Successful With Marketing*

Ace McCloud

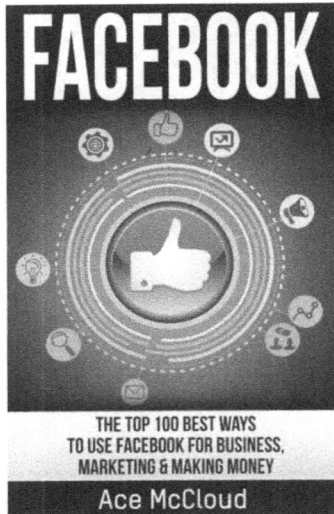

FACEBOOK

THE TOP 100 BEST WAYS
TO USE FACEBOOK FOR BUSINESS,
MARKETING & MAKING MONEY

Ace McCloud

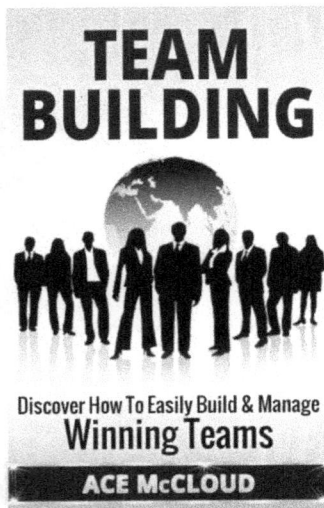

**TEAM
BUILDING**

Discover How To Easily Build & Manage
Winning Teams

ACE McCLOUD

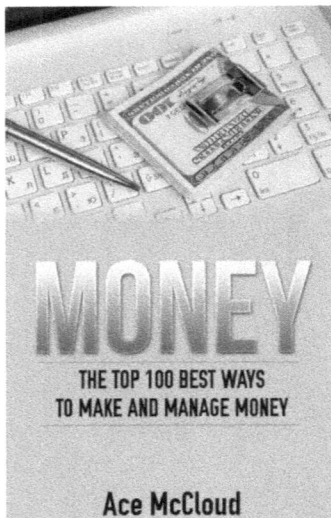

MONEY

THE TOP 100 BEST WAYS
TO MAKE AND MANAGE MONEY

Ace McCloud

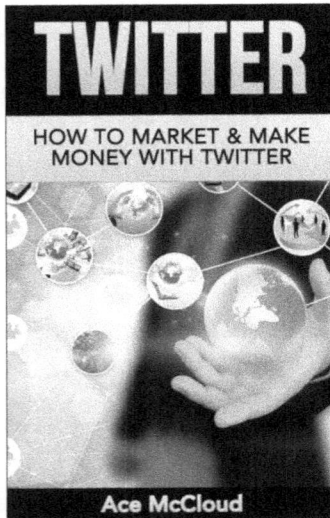

TWITTER

HOW TO MARKET & MAKE
MONEY WITH TWITTER

Ace McCloud

COMMUNICATION SKILLS

Discover The Best Ways To Communicate,
Be Charismatic, Use Body Language,
Persuade & Be A Great Conversationalist

Ace McCloud

YouTube

THE TOP 100 BEST WAYS
TO MARKET & MAKE MONEY WITH YOUTUBE

Ace McCloud

Peak Performance Books

SUCCESS

SUCCESS STRATEGIES

THE TOP 100 BEST WAYS TO BE SUCCESSFUL

Ace McCloud

Ace McCloud

HABIT

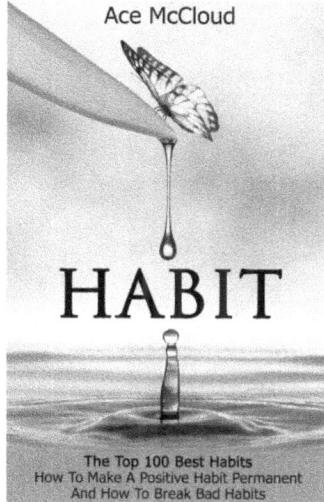

The Top 100 Best Habits
How To Make A Positive Habit Permanent
And How To Break Bad Habits

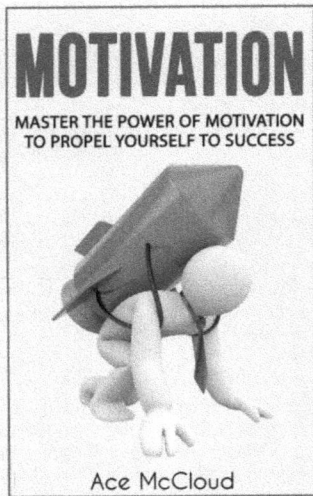

MOTIVATION

MASTER THE POWER OF MOTIVATION
TO PROPEL YOURSELF TO SUCCESS

Ace McCloud

ATTITUDE

Discover The True Power Of
A Positive Attitude

Ace McCloud

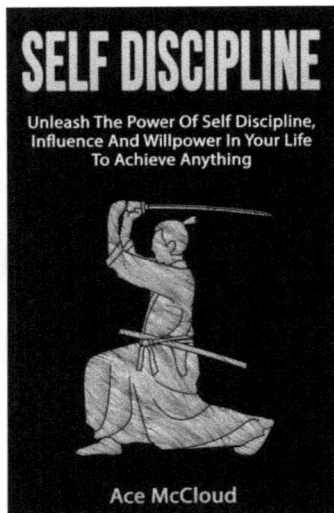

SELF DISCIPLINE

Unleash The Power Of Self Discipline,
Influence And Willpower In Your Life
To Achieve Anything

Ace McCloud

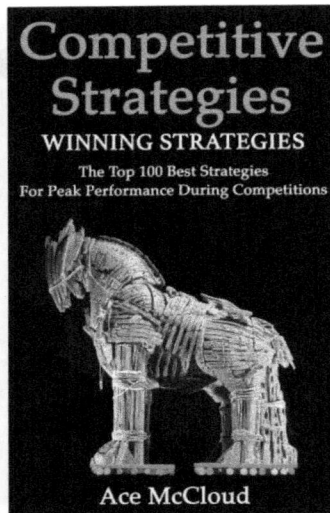

Competitive Strategies

WINNING STRATEGIES

The Top 100 Best Strategies
For Peak Performance During Competitions

Ace McCloud

Be sure to check out my audio books as well!

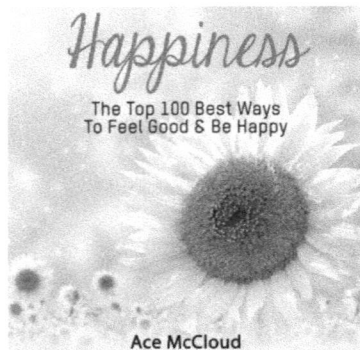

Happiness

The Top 100 Best Ways
To Feel Good & Be Happy

Ace McCloud

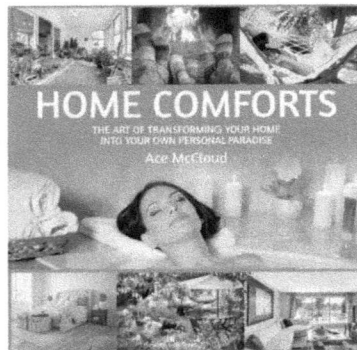

HOME COMFORTS

THE ART OF TRANSFORMING YOUR HOME
INTO YOUR OWN PERSONAL PARADISE

Ace McCloud

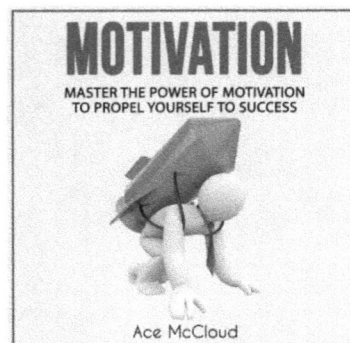

MOTIVATION

MASTER THE POWER OF MOTIVATION
TO PROPEL YOURSELF TO SUCCESS

Ace McCloud

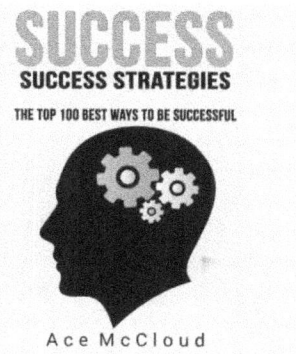

Check out my website at: **www.AcesEbooks.com** for a complete list of all of my books and high quality audio books. I enjoy bringing you the best knowledge in the world and wish you the best in using this information to make your journey through life better and more enjoyable! **Best of luck to you!**

www.ingramcontent.com/pod-product-compliance
Lightning Source LLC
Chambersburg PA
CBHW081555220326
41598CB00036B/6681